EMMANUEL JOSEPH

The Symphony of Speech, Orchestrating Voice, Gesture, and Silence for Maximum Impact

Copyright © 2025 by Emmanuel Joseph

All rights reserved. No part of this publication may be reproduced, stored or transmitted in any form or by any means, electronic, mechanical, photocopying, recording, scanning, or otherwise without written permission from the publisher. It is illegal to copy this book, post it to a website, or distribute it by any other means without permission.

First edition

This book was professionally typeset on Reedsy. Find out more at reedsy.com

Contents

1	Chapter 1: The Conductor's Baton – The Power of Voice	1
2	Chapter 2: The Dance of Hands – The Language of Gesture	3
3	Chapter 3: The Pause That Resonates – The Art of Silence	5
4	Chapter 4: The Harmony of Voice and Gesture	7
5	Chapter 5: The Trio of Impact – Voice, Gesture, and Silence	9
6	Chapter 6: The Audience as the Orchestra – Understanding...	11
7	Chapter 7: The Crescendo – Building Momentum in Your Speech	13
8	Chapter 8: The Tempo of Connection – Pacing Your Speech	15
9	Chapter 9: The Dynamics of Emotion – Harnessing Feeling in...	17
10	Chapter 10: The Universal Language – Adapting to Cultural...	19
11	Chapter 11: The Improvisation of Authenticity – Speaking...	21
12	Chapter 12: The Encore – Leaving a Lasting Impression	23
13	Epilogue: The Maestro Within – Mastering the Symphony of...	24

1

Chapter 1: The Conductor's Baton – The Power of Voice

The human voice is the foundation of communication, a tool as versatile as it is profound. It carries not only words but also emotions, intentions, and energy. A well-modulated voice can inspire, comfort, or command attention, while a flat or monotonous tone can render even the most brilliant ideas forgettable. The key lies in understanding the nuances of pitch, pace, and volume. A speaker who masters these elements can create a rhythm that resonates with their audience, much like a conductor leading an orchestra.

Voice is not just about sound; it's about connection. When you speak, your voice becomes a bridge between your inner world and the listener's. A warm, confident tone can foster trust, while a hesitant or shrill voice may create distance. The art of speech lies in aligning your voice with your message, ensuring that every word is delivered with intention. Whether you're addressing a crowd or having a one-on-one conversation, your voice is your most immediate instrument for impact.

Yet, the power of voice extends beyond mere delivery. It is also about authenticity. People can sense when a voice is forced or insincere, and this dissonance can undermine even the most well-crafted message. To truly connect, your voice must reflect your true self, carrying the weight of your convictions and the sincerity of your emotions. This authenticity is what transforms speech from mere noise into a symphony of meaning.

Practice is essential to harnessing the full potential of your voice. Just as a musician rehearses scales, a speaker must experiment with tone, inflection, and pacing. Record yourself, listen critically, and refine your delivery. Over time, you'll develop a voice that is not only powerful but also uniquely yours. Remember, the goal is not perfection but resonance—creating a sound that moves and inspires.

In the symphony of speech, the voice is the melody. It carries the tune, but it must be supported by other elements to achieve its full effect. As we explore the interplay of voice, gesture, and silence, remember that each component is essential. Together, they create a harmony that can captivate, persuade, and transform.

2

Chapter 2: The Dance of Hands – The Language of Gesture

Gestures are the silent partners of speech, adding depth and dimension to your words. They can emphasize a point, convey emotion, or even replace words altogether. A well-timed gesture can make your message more memorable, while a clumsy or excessive movement can distract or confuse. The key is to use gestures purposefully, ensuring they enhance rather than detract from your speech.

The language of gesture is universal, transcending cultural and linguistic barriers. A raised hand can signal a pause, a nod can express agreement, and an open palm can convey honesty. These nonverbal cues are processed instinctively by the brain, often before the words themselves are fully understood. This makes gestures a powerful tool for reinforcing your message and building rapport with your audience.

However, gestures must be natural and aligned with your personality. Forced or exaggerated movements can come across as insincere, undermining your credibility. The best gestures are those that flow organically from your emotions and intentions. They should feel like an extension of your voice, amplifying your message without overshadowing it.

To master the art of gesture, observe yourself in action. Pay attention to how your hands move when you speak, and identify any habits that might detract from your message. Practice in front of a mirror or with a trusted friend, refining your movements until they feel effortless and authentic. Over time, you'll develop a repertoire of gestures that enhance your speech and engage your audience.

In the symphony of speech, gestures are the rhythm section. They provide structure and momentum, guiding the listener through your message. When used effectively, they can transform a monologue into a dynamic performance, leaving a lasting impression on your audience.

3

Chapter 3: The Pause That Resonates – The Art of Silence

Silence is often overlooked in the art of speech, yet it is one of the most powerful tools at a speaker's disposal. A well-placed pause can create suspense, emphasize a point, or give the audience time to reflect. It is the space between the notes that gives music its beauty, and the same is true for speech. Silence allows your words to breathe, making them more impactful and memorable.

The art of silence lies in its timing. A pause that is too short may go unnoticed, while one that is too long can feel awkward or unsettling. The key is to use silence strategically, letting it enhance your message without disrupting the flow of your speech. A pause before a key point can build anticipation, while a pause after can allow the idea to sink in.

Silence also serves as a mirror, reflecting the emotions and reactions of your audience. It gives them time to process your words and connect with your message on a deeper level. In this way, silence becomes a form of dialogue, creating a shared experience between speaker and listener.

To master the art of silence, practice incorporating pauses into your speech. Pay attention to how they affect the rhythm and impact of your words. Experiment with different lengths and placements, and observe how your audience responds. Over time, you'll develop an intuitive sense of when and how to use silence for maximum effect.

In the symphony of speech, silence is the rest note. It may seem like nothing, but it is essential to the overall composition. When used skillfully, it can elevate your speech from ordinary to extraordinary, leaving a lasting impression on your audience.

4

Chapter 4: The Harmony of Voice and Gesture

Voice and gesture are two sides of the same coin, each enhancing the other to create a cohesive and compelling message. When used in harmony, they can amplify your impact, making your speech more engaging and memorable. The key is to ensure that your gestures align with your words, reinforcing rather than contradicting your message.

For example, a passionate statement paired with a clenched fist can convey determination, while a gentle tone accompanied by open palms can express empathy. The synergy between voice and gesture creates a multisensory experience for your audience, engaging both their ears and their eyes. This dual-channel communication makes your message more persuasive and easier to remember.

However, achieving this harmony requires practice and self-awareness. Pay attention to how your gestures align with your voice, and make adjustments as needed. Avoid repetitive or distracting movements, and ensure that your gestures are purposeful and meaningful. The goal is to create a seamless blend of voice and gesture that enhances your message without overwhelming it.

To refine this harmony, record yourself speaking and observe how your gestures complement your voice. Seek feedback from others, and be open to making changes. Over time, you'll develop a natural synergy between your

THE SYMPHONY OF SPEECH, ORCHESTRATING VOICE, GESTURE, AND SILENCE FOR MAXIMUM IMPACT

voice and gestures, creating a dynamic and impactful speaking style.

In the symphony of speech, voice and gesture are the melody and rhythm. Together, they create a rich and textured performance that captivates and inspires. When used in harmony, they can transform your speech into a masterpiece of communication.

5

Chapter 5: The Trio of Impact – Voice, Gesture, and Silence

The true power of speech lies in the interplay of voice, gesture, and silence. Each element has its role, but it is their combination that creates maximum impact. Like a musical trio, they must work together in perfect harmony, each enhancing the others to create a cohesive and compelling performance.

Voice carries the message, gesture adds depth and dimension, and silence provides space for reflection. Together, they create a dynamic and engaging experience for your audience. The key is to balance these elements, ensuring that none dominates or detracts from the others. A well-timed pause can make a gesture more meaningful, while a powerful gesture can give weight to your words.

To master this trio, practice integrating voice, gesture, and silence into your speech. Pay attention to how they interact, and make adjustments as needed. Experiment with different combinations, and observe how your audience responds. Over time, you'll develop an intuitive sense of how to balance these elements for maximum impact.

In the symphony of speech, voice, gesture, and silence are the essential instruments. When played together in harmony, they create a performance that is both powerful and unforgettable. By mastering this trio, you can elevate your speech to new heights, leaving a lasting impression on your audience.

6

Chapter 6: The Audience as the Orchestra – Understanding Your Listeners

Every speech is a dialogue, even when only one person is speaking. The audience plays a crucial role in the symphony of speech, reacting to your words, gestures, and pauses in real time. To truly connect, you must understand your listeners—their needs, expectations, and emotions. This understanding allows you to tailor your message, ensuring it resonates deeply and leaves a lasting impact.

Begin by researching your audience. What are their interests, values, and concerns? What do they hope to gain from your speech? This knowledge will help you craft a message that speaks directly to them, making your words more relevant and engaging. Remember, a speech that resonates with one audience may fall flat with another. Adaptability is key.

During your speech, pay attention to nonverbal cues from your audience. Are they leaning forward, nodding, or smiling? These are signs of engagement. Conversely, crossed arms, fidgeting, or blank stares may indicate disinterest or confusion. Use these cues to adjust your delivery, emphasizing key points or clarifying complex ideas.

Empathy is the bridge between speaker and audience. Put yourself in their shoes, and consider how your message will be received. Speak to their hearts as well as their minds, using stories, humor, or shared experiences to create a sense of connection. When your audience feels understood, they are more likely to trust and engage with you.

In the symphony of speech, the audience is the orchestra. They respond to your cues, adding their own energy and emotion to the performance. By understanding and engaging them, you create a shared experience that is both powerful and memorable.

7

Chapter 7: The Crescendo – Building Momentum in Your Speech

A great speech is like a musical composition, with peaks and valleys that guide the listener through a journey. The crescendo—the gradual buildup of intensity—is a powerful tool for maintaining interest and driving your message home. By structuring your speech to build momentum, you can captivate your audience and leave them inspired.

Start with a strong opening that grabs attention and sets the tone. This could be a compelling story, a surprising fact, or a thought-provoking question. Your opening should hint at the journey ahead, drawing your audience in and making them eager to hear more.

As you move through your speech, vary the pace and intensity to keep your audience engaged. Alternate between moments of high energy and quieter, reflective pauses. This ebb and flow creates a dynamic rhythm that holds attention and prevents monotony. Use your voice, gestures, and silence to emphasize key points, building toward the climax of your speech.

The climax is the emotional peak of your speech, the moment when your message hits home. This is where you deliver your most powerful words, supported by your most expressive gestures and pauses. Make it count. The climax should leave your audience moved, inspired, or motivated to act.

Finally, end with a strong conclusion that reinforces your message and

THE SYMPHONY OF SPEECH, ORCHESTRATING VOICE, GESTURE, AND SILENCE FOR MAXIMUM IMPACT

leaves a lasting impression. This could be a call to action, a poignant story, or a memorable quote. Your closing should feel satisfying, like the final chord of a symphony, bringing your speech to a harmonious close.

In the symphony of speech, the crescendo is the driving force that carries your audience along. By building momentum and delivering a powerful climax, you create a speech that is both engaging and unforgettable.

8

Chapter 8: The Tempo of Connection – Pacing Your Speech

Pacing is the heartbeat of your speech, determining its rhythm and flow. Too fast, and your audience may struggle to keep up. Too slow, and they may lose interest. The key is to find the right tempo—one that matches your message and engages your listeners.

Start by considering the complexity of your content. Simple ideas can be delivered quickly, while complex concepts may require a slower pace and more pauses for reflection. Adjust your tempo to suit the needs of your audience, ensuring they can follow and absorb your message.

Your voice is a powerful tool for controlling pace. Use variations in speed to create excitement, emphasize key points, or signal transitions. A sudden slowdown can draw attention to an important idea, while a quickened pace can convey urgency or enthusiasm. Experiment with different tempos to find what works best for your message.

Gestures and silence also play a role in pacing. A well-timed gesture can punctuate a point, while a pause can give your audience time to process what you've said. Use these elements to break up your speech, creating a rhythm that feels natural and engaging.

Practice is essential to mastering pacing. Record yourself speaking, and listen for moments where the tempo feels off. Seek feedback from others,

THE SYMPHONY OF SPEECH, ORCHESTRATING VOICE, GESTURE, AND SILENCE FOR MAXIMUM IMPACT

and make adjustments as needed. Over time, you'll develop an intuitive sense of how to pace your speech for maximum impact.

In the symphony of speech, pacing is the tempo that keeps your audience engaged. By finding the right rhythm, you create a speech that flows smoothly and holds attention from start to finish.

9

Chapter 9: The Dynamics of Emotion – Harnessing Feeling in Your Speech

Emotion is the soul of speech, transforming words into a powerful force that moves and inspires. Whether it's joy, anger, sadness, or hope, emotion connects you with your audience on a deep, human level. To harness this power, you must tap into your own feelings and convey them authentically through your voice, gestures, and silence.

Begin by identifying the emotional core of your message. What do you want your audience to feel? Once you've clarified this, use your voice to convey the appropriate emotion. A warm, gentle tone can express compassion, while a sharp, forceful tone can convey urgency or determination. Let your voice reflect the depth of your feelings, creating an emotional resonance with your listeners.

Gestures are another powerful tool for expressing emotion. A clenched fist can convey determination, while open palms can express vulnerability or honesty. Use your body to amplify the emotional content of your words, creating a multisensory experience for your audience.

Silence, too, can be deeply emotional. A pause can create suspense, allowing your audience to anticipate what's coming next. It can also give them time to process and feel the weight of your words. Use silence strategically to heighten the emotional impact of your speech.

THE SYMPHONY OF SPEECH, ORCHESTRATING VOICE, GESTURE, AND SILENCE FOR MAXIMUM IMPACT

To master the dynamics of emotion, practice speaking with feeling. Record yourself, and listen for moments where your emotion shines through. Seek feedback from others, and refine your delivery to ensure your feelings come across authentically.

In the symphony of speech, emotion is the melody that touches the heart. By harnessing the power of feeling, you create a speech that is not only heard but also felt.

10

Chapter 10: The Universal Language – Adapting to Cultural Contexts

Speech is a universal language, but its nuances vary across cultures. Gestures, tone, and even silence can carry different meanings depending on the cultural context. To communicate effectively, you must adapt your speech to resonate with diverse audiences, respecting their norms and values.

Begin by researching the cultural background of your audience. What gestures are considered polite or offensive? How do they perceive tone and volume? This knowledge will help you avoid misunderstandings and build rapport with your listeners.

Be mindful of nonverbal cues, as they can vary widely across cultures. For example, direct eye contact may be seen as confident in some cultures but disrespectful in others. Similarly, a gesture that is positive in one context may be negative in another. Adapt your gestures to align with the cultural norms of your audience.

Tone and pacing also play a role in cross-cultural communication. Some cultures prefer a formal, measured tone, while others respond better to a casual, energetic delivery. Adjust your style to match the expectations of your audience, ensuring your message is received as intended.

Finally, embrace cultural diversity as an opportunity to learn and grow.

THE SYMPHONY OF SPEECH, ORCHESTRATING VOICE, GESTURE, AND SILENCE FOR MAXIMUM IMPACT

By adapting your speech to different contexts, you not only enhance your effectiveness as a speaker but also deepen your understanding of the world.

In the symphony of speech, cultural awareness is the key to universal harmony. By respecting and adapting to cultural differences, you create a speech that resonates across borders and boundaries.

11

Chapter 11: The Improvisation of Authenticity – Speaking from the Heart

While preparation is essential, the most impactful speeches often include moments of spontaneity and authenticity. These unscripted moments allow you to connect with your audience on a deeper level, revealing your true self and creating a sense of shared humanity.

Authenticity begins with self-awareness. Know your values, beliefs, and passions, and let them shine through in your speech. Speak from the heart, sharing personal stories or insights that reflect your genuine self. This vulnerability creates trust and fosters a deeper connection with your audience.

Improvisation is the art of thinking on your feet, responding to the moment with creativity and confidence. This might mean adjusting your speech based on audience reactions, incorporating a spontaneous story, or addressing an unexpected question. Embrace these moments as opportunities to connect and engage.

To cultivate authenticity and improvisation, practice speaking without a script. Focus on your core message, and trust yourself to express it in your own words. Over time, you'll develop the confidence and flexibility to speak from the heart, even in high-pressure situations.

In the symphony of speech, authenticity is the soulful solo that stands out.

THE SYMPHONY OF SPEECH, ORCHESTRATING VOICE, GESTURE, AND SILENCE FOR MAXIMUM IMPACT

By speaking from the heart and embracing spontaneity, you create a speech that is not only impactful but also deeply human.

12

Chapter 12: The Encore – Leaving a Lasting Impression

The end of your speech is not the end of its impact. A great speech lingers in the minds and hearts of your audience, inspiring them to think, feel, or act differently. To achieve this, you must craft a conclusion that resonates and leaves a lasting impression.

Your closing should reinforce your core message, tying together the themes and ideas you've explored. This could be a powerful statement, a call to action, or a memorable story. Whatever form it takes, your conclusion should feel satisfying and complete, like the final note of a symphony.

Use your voice, gestures, and silence to emphasize your closing words. A strong, confident tone can convey conviction, while a gentle, reflective tone can leave your audience with a sense of warmth and inspiration. A well-timed pause can give your final words added weight, allowing them to sink in.

Finally, end with gratitude. Thank your audience for their time and attention, acknowledging the role they've played in the shared experience of your speech. This gesture of appreciation creates a positive final impression, leaving your audience feeling valued and respected.

In the symphony of speech, the encore is the moment that lingers. By crafting a powerful conclusion and expressing gratitude, you create a speech that resonates long after the final word is spoken.

13

Epilogue: The Maestro Within – Mastering the Symphony of Speech

The art of speech is a lifelong journey, one that requires practice, reflection, and a willingness to grow. As you refine your voice, gestures, and use of silence, you'll discover the maestro within—the part of you that can orchestrate words and emotions into a symphony of impact.

Remember, the goal is not perfection but connection. Each speech is an opportunity to learn, to connect, and to inspire. Embrace the process, and trust in your ability to create something beautiful.

In the end, the symphony of speech is not just about words. It's about the human connection that words can create. By mastering this art, you have the power to move, inspire, and transform the world—one speech at a time.

Book Description:

The Symphony of Speech: Orchestrating Voice, Gesture, and Silence for Maximum Impact is a transformative guide to mastering the art of communication. This book is not just about speaking—it's about creating a powerful, resonant connection with your audience through the harmonious interplay of voice, gesture, and silence.

Imagine your words as notes, your gestures as rhythm, and your pauses as the spaces between the music. Together, they form a symphony that can

EPILOGUE: THE MAESTRO WITHIN – MASTERING THE SYMPHONY OF...

captivate, inspire, and move people to action. This book takes you on a journey through the essential elements of impactful communication, offering practical techniques, insightful strategies, and real-world examples to help you refine your craft.

From understanding the nuances of your voice to harnessing the silent power of gestures and pauses, each chapter builds on the last, guiding you toward a deeper understanding of how to connect with any audience. You'll learn how to adapt to cultural contexts, build emotional resonance, and leave a lasting impression that extends far beyond your final word.

Whether you're a seasoned speaker or just starting out, *The Symphony of Speech* will empower you to communicate with confidence, authenticity, and impact. It's not just a book—it's an invitation to step into your role as a maestro of communication, crafting speeches that resonate, inspire, and transform.

www.ingramcontent.com/pod-product-compliance
Lightning Source LLC
LaVergne TN
LVHW020744090526
838202LV00057BA/6224